D1267043

REMARKABLE REPTILES

LIZARDS

WITHDRAWN

James E. Gerholdt

WITHDRAWN

Published by Abdo & Daughters, 4940 Viking Drive, Suite 622, Edina, Minnesota 55435.

Library bound edition distributed by Rockbottom Books, Pentagon Tower, P.O. Box 36036, Minneapolis, Minnesota 55435.

Copyright © 1994 by Abdo Consulting Group, Inc., Pentagon Tower, P.O. Box 36036, Minneapolis, Minnesota 55435 USA. International copyrights reserved in all countries. No part of this book may be reproduced in any form without written permission from the publisher.

Printed in the United States.

Cover Photo credit: Peter Arnold
Interior Photo credits: James Gerholdt, pages 5, 7, 9, 11, 13, 15, 17, 21
Barney Oldfield, page 21
Peter Arnold, pages 6, 9
Photos courtesy of Rebecca Heller, pages 5 and 9

Edited By: Julie Berg

LIBRARY OF CONGRESS CATALOGING-IN-PUBLICATION DATA

Gerholdt, James E., 1943—
    Lizards / James E. Gerholdt.
        p.   cm. -- (Remarkable Reptiles)
    Includes glossary and index.
    ISBN 1-56239-306-5
    1. Lizards--Juvenile literature.   [1. Lizards.] I. Title. II. Series.
    QL666.L2G46   1994
    597.95--dc20   94-6355
                                          CIP
                                          AC

CONTENTS

LIZARDS

Lizards are reptiles. Reptiles are ectothermic. This means they get their body temperature from the environment, either from lying in the sun or on a warm rock. Lizards like it warm. Most like temperatures from 75 to 85 degrees Fahrenheit, and some like it even warmer. If they get too hot, they will die and if they are too cold, their bodies won't work. There are more than 3,500 species of lizards. They are found almost everywhere in the world.

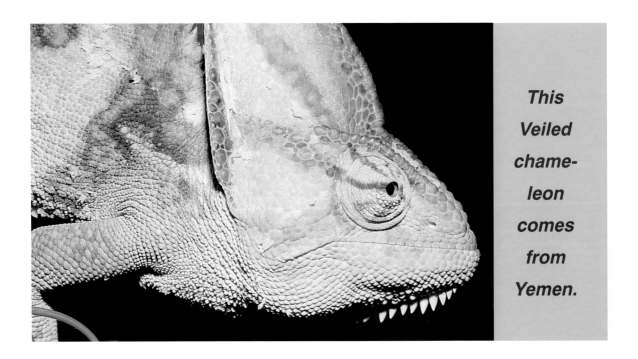

This Veiled chameleon comes from Yemen.

The Leopard gecko comes from India and Pakistan.

The Blue-tongued skink comes from New Guinea.

SIZES

Some lizards are giants. The Komodo dragon lizard from Indonesia can be 10 feet long and weigh 300 pounds. But it is not the longest lizard. The Crocodile monitor from New Guinea has been reported up to 13 feet long, but it is not as heavy as the Komodo dragon lizard. The smallest lizard in the world is a gecko from South America. An adult gecko may be less than 2 inches long! Most lizards are not this small, and measure from 6 to 24 inches long.

The Komodo dragon is a giant lizard.

This Texas banded gecko is only 3 inches long.

SHAPES

Lizards come in many different shapes. Some are long and slender and some are short and fat. Most lizards have four legs, but some have only two. The legs may be long or short. The toes usually have claws, but some have suction cups instead. And some lizards don't have any legs at all! The tails of most lizards are about the same length as the body, but on certain types, like the glass lizards, can be twice as long as the body. The Green iguana has a row of crests on its back.

You can see the claws on the foot of this Veiled Chame-leon.

The Frilled lizard from Australia has a neck that flares out when it is scared.

The European glass lizard has no legs.

This male Collared lizard is brightly colored.

COLORS

Many lizards are very colorful, just about any color you could imagine. Others, like the desert lizards, have shades that help them blend in with their surroundings. This is called camouflage. Male lizards of some species have bright colors, the females are plain. Collared lizards are a good example of this. But, both male and female skinks and whiptails are colored the same.

This female Reticulate collared lizard is hard to see.

The Reticulate collared lizard lives on rocky hillsides.

HABITAT

Lizards live in many different kinds of habitats. Some live near rocks, so they can sun themselves or hide. Other types enjoy sandy deserts where they can bury themselves in the sand. Jungles and rain forests are home to many different species of lizards. Here they can run up the trees or hide on the forest floor. Some lizards spend most of their time in the water. Every species of lizard has its own needs.

The Texas spotted whiptail lives in the desert.

The Leopard gecko has keen eyesight.

SENSES

Lizards have the same five senses as humans. Most of them have very good eyesight and can see for a long distance. They can see their enemies before it is too late. All lizards can hear, and only a few make any noise other than a hiss. But some geckos can squeak or bark! Lizards smell with their tongues. This sense is very important to them and helps them to find their food.

The Tokay gecko uses its tongue to smell.

DEFENSE

One way a lizard defends itself is to run away from its enemies. Lizards can run up to 18 miles per hour! The Zebra-tailed lizard has been clocked at this speed. Some, like the Collared lizards, actually get up on their hind legs to run like a human! Many lizards lose their tail to get away quickly. But don't worry. The lizard can grow a new one! Many lizards open their mouths and look fierce, and some can bite hard. The horned lizards have sharp horns and scales to make it hard for animals to swallow them.

The horns on this Texas horned lizard are sharp.

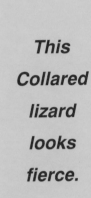

This Collared lizard looks fierce.

This Great plains skink can bite hard.

FOOD

Lizards eat just about everything. Some eat only fruits and vegetables while others eat only insects and other live food. A few lizards eat all of the above and are called omnivorous. Very large lizards can eat birds and other animals. The Komodo dragon lizard eats pigs and deer, and sometimes people! Chameleons can use their tongue to snatch insects from branches several inches away.

This Blue-tongued skink is about to eat an apple.

This European glass lizard is eating a small mouse.

BABIES

Most lizard babies hatch from eggs. The eggs are laid under rocks, or in holes in the ground. Some species of geckos lay eggs on trees or even on houses. Regardless of where they are laid, it usually takes 2 to 3 months for the eggs to hatch. Some species of lizards may lay only one egg, while other lizards may lay many more. Some lizards, like the Blue-tongued skink, give birth to tiny live babies which are on their own as soon as they are born. Very few lizard mothers have anything to do with their babies once they are born.

This Prairie skink is full of eggs. See how lumpy she is?

Here are some lizard eggs just laid.

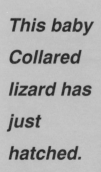

This baby Collared lizard has just hatched.

GLOSSARY

Camouflage (CAM-o-flaj) - The ability to blend in with the surroundings.

Ectothermic (ek-to-THERM-ik) - Regulating body temperature from an outside heat source.

Environment (en-VI-ron-ment) - Surroundings an animal lives in.

Habitat (HAB-e-tat) - An area an animal lives in.

Omnivorous (om-NIV-or-us) - An animal that eats both plant and animal matter.

Reptiles (REP-tiles) - Scaly-skinned animals with backbones.

Species (SPES-es) - A kind or type.

Suction cups - Things that stick to a smooth surface.

Index

About the Author

Jim Gerholdt has been studying reptiles and amphibians for more than 40 years. He has presented lectures and displays throughout the state of Minnesota for 9 years. He is a founding member of the Minnesota Herpetological Society and is active in conservation issues involving reptiles and amphibians in India and Aruba, as well as Minnesota.

Photo by Tim Judy

J597.95
G

WITHDRAWN
Community Library